Editor-in-Chief and Founder:
  Lyndon H. LaRouche, Jr.
Editorial Board: *Lyndon H. LaRouche, Jr., Helga
  Zepp-LaRouche, Robert Ingraham, Tony
  Papert, Gerald Rose, Dennis Small, Jeffrey
  Steinberg, William Wertz*
Co-Editors: *Robert Ingraham, Tony Papert*
Managing Editor: *Nancy Spannaus*
Technology: *Marsha Freeman*
Books: *Katherine Notley*
Ebooks: *Richard Burden*
Graphics: *Alan Yue*
Photos: *Stuart Lewis*
Circulation Manager: *Stanley Ezrol*

INTELLIGENCE DIRECTORS
Counterintelligence: *Jeffrey Steinberg, Michele
  Steinberg*
Economics: *John Hoefle, Marcia Merry Baker,
  Paul Gallagher*
History: *Anton Chaitkin*
Ibero-America: *Dennis Small*
Russia and Eastern Europe: *Rachel Douglas*
United States: *Debra Freeman*

INTERNATIONAL BUREAUS
Bogotá: *Miriam Redondo*
Berlin: *Rainer Apel*
Copenhagen: *Tom Gillesberg*
Houston: *Harley Schlanger*
Lima: *Sara Madueño*
Melbourne: *Robert Barwick*
Mexico City: *Gerardo Castilleja Chávez*
New Delhi: *Ramtanu Maitra*
Paris: *Christine Bierre*
Stockholm: *Ulf Sandmark*
United Nations, N.Y.C.: *Leni Rubinstein*
Washington, D.C.: *William Jones*
Wiesbaden: *Göran Haglund*

ON THE WEB
e-mail: eirns@larouchepub.com
www.larouchepub.com
www.executiveintelligencereview.com
www.larouchepub.com/eiw
Webmaster: *John Sigerson*
Assistant Webmaster: *George Hollis*
Editor, Arabic-language edition: *Hussein Askary*

EIR (ISSN 0273-6314) *is published weekly
(50 issues), by EIR News Service, Inc.,
P.O. Box 17390, Washington, D.C. 20041-0390.
(703) 777-9451 ext. 415*

European Headquarters: E.I.R. GmbH, Postfach
Bahnstrasse 9a, D-65205, Wiesbaden, Germany
Tel: 49-611-73650
Homepage: http://www.eirna.com
e-mail: eirna@eirna.com
Director: Georg Neudecker

Montreal, Canada: 514-461-1557

Denmark: EIR - Danmark, Sankt Knuds Vej 11,
basement left, DK-1903 Frederiksberg, Denmark.
Tel.: +45 35 43 60 40, Fax: +45 35 43 87 57. e-mail:
eirdk@hotmail.com.

Mexico City: EIR, Sor Juana Inés de la Cruz 242-2
Col. Agricultura C.P. 11360
Delegación M. Hidalgo, México D.F.
Tel. (5525) 5318-2301
eirmexico@gmail.com

Canada Post Publication Sales Agreement
#40683579

Postmaster: Send all address changes to *EIR*, P.O.
Box 17390, Washington, D.C. 20041-0390.

Signed articles in *EIR* represent the views of the
authors, and not necessarily those of the Editorial
Board.

The Moment of Decision

EIR Contents

www.larouchepub.com Volume 43, Number 39, September 23, 2016

Cover This Week

The Great Hall of the United Nations General Assembly

www.unodc.org

I. Which Future Will We Choose?

APPEAL TO THE UNITED NATIONS GENERAL ASSEMBLY

A New Paradigm for the Common Aims of Mankind!

by Helga Zepp-LaRouche

Sept. 16—It is crucial that the General Assembly of the United Nations, now convening in New York, build on the progress that the G-20 Summit has achieved under China's leadership. That summit has set a course toward a new financial architecture, and the chance is greater than ever that all nations can participate in the building of the New Silk Road on the basis of "win-win" cooperation, and that the productivity of the world economy will rise on the basis of innovation, thus overcoming poverty and the consequences of war.

The main problem, however, is that the West continues to cling to the status quo of a uni-polar world and the neo-liberal financial system, although both of those objectives have been unachievable for along time. The rise of Asia signifies that one nation will no longer be able to set the rules, and therefore solutions must be found through dialogue and negotiation. The neo-liberal system is in the throes of an existential crisis.

The first tactic of the globalized uni-polar outlook, the policy of regime-change and alleged humanitarian interventions, has cost the lives of millions of people, brought untold suffering to millions more, destroyed entire regions, thus creating the breeding grounds for the spread of terrorism, and has set off huge waves of refugees.

The wars against Iraq and Afghanistan alone, according to the study of Professor Neta Crawford of Brown University, have cost five trillion dollars, and have yielded this devastating result.

The second tactic of the globalized uni-polar world has been to maximize the profits for the banks which are supposedly too big to be allowed to fail (TBTF). This has led to an unbearable gap between rich and poor. The TBTF banks, with their insufficient capital base, must pay the full sum of their fines for criminal

UN General Assembly hall at the UN Headquarters in New York City.

methods, and declare bankruptcy, instead of being bailed out.

Now, a new meltdown threatens, with even more catastrophic consequences than the collapse of Lehman Brothers in 2008, because central bank schemes and methods of financial manipulations have been exhausted and are no longer effective.

In that context, two reports released in Great Britain offer an extraordinary opportunity to re-assess and correct the current policy. After the Chilcot Report, which laid the blame on Tony Blair for the illegal Iraq war which was built on lies, a commission of the British Parliament has levelled no less scathing charges against former Prime Minister David Cameron for the war in Libya, which was carried out on erroneous assumptions and led to political and economic collapse, inter-militia and inter-tribal warfare, humanitarian and migrant crises, widespread human rights violations, the spread of Qaddafi regime weapons across the region, and the growth of ISIL in North Africa.

On the role of the United States, the report states that, "The United States was instrumental in extending the terms of Resolution 1973 beyond the imposition of a no-fly zone to include the authorization of all necessary measures to protect civilians. In practice, this led to the imposition of a no-drive zone and the assumed authority to attack the entire Libyan Government command and communications network."

That same overall review of the current policy should, of course, include the implications of the 28 pages of the official Joint Congressional Inquiry Report, which deals with the circumstances of the attacks of Sept. 11, 2001, as well as the JASTA bill, which necessitate a completely new investigation.

This failed policy has caused:

• the millions of dead and injured

• the traumatized children and soldiers (including in the nations waging war)

www.panafricanistinternational.org
Misrata, Libya, Sept. 17, 2011, during the NATO assault on Libya.

Prime Minister David Cameron announcing his resignation on June 24, 2016.

RT screen grab

• the destruction of cities, villages, infrastructure and irreplaceable cultural wealth.

In light of this horrendous suffering, it is not only appropriate, but a moral obligation for the countries that took part in these wars in the different coalitions of the willing, to examine the political process in their parliaments and to fully participate in the reconstruction of the regions that have been devastated. This will not bring the dead back to life, but the admission of guilt and a genuine change of policy towards development would give the people living there today hope for a future.

The status quo cannot be maintained. As a result of both policies of globalization, there has been an enormous loss of trust among the populations in the trans-Atlantic world. Right-wing populist and right-extremist parties are rapidly gaining strength. The conditions of the 1930s threaten to reappear in a new form, the European Union is crumbling, and the refugee crisis will not be solved by securing the external EU borders, but will only force refugees to be relocated and removed from the news. The U.S. economy is collapsing, while the society is more than ever torn and overtaken by violence. Either this process will lead to an escalation of the confrontation with Russia and China, and to the extermination of mankind in a great war, or the leading politicians in the West will have to have the moral integrity to correct the errors of the past.

The Solution

To come back to the positive proposition at the beginning of this appeal, the course has been set toward a way out of this crisis of civilization since the G-20 summit.

beyase.org

China standard gauge railway project in Kenya that will be part of a six-nation East African regional rail network.

Not only has China presented a new level of cooperation that is not based on geopolitics, but rather on a policy that is in the mutual interest of all. It has also pledged to industrialize Africa and other low-income countries, an approach that could both solve the refugee crisis and eliminate the terrorist environment. Clearly, the extension of the New Silk Road to the Middle East and Africa both requires and will bring about growth rates of seven to ten percent.

The Club of Rome has promptly stepped in with a new report under the cynical title of *One Percent Is Enough,* which would lead to population reduction, a fascist policy for which the Club of Rome is infamous. The UN recently emphasized that Africa needs a growth rate of at least seven to eight percent. When one of the authors of the Club of Rome report, the Norwegian Jorgen Randers, made the absurd statement that "My daughter is the most dangerous animal in the world, because she consumes 30 times more energy than a girl in a developing country," it reveals the bestial image of man on which the Club of Rome bases its argument.

Man, in contrast to all other creatures, is able to use his creative potential to continually discover new insights into the laws of the universe. This is called scientific progress. The unlimited process of perfecting the human mind corresponds with the laws of the physical universe, which develops to ever higher energy-flux densities. We are not in a closed system on the Earth, as the Club of Rome and similar organizations claim, but rather, our planet is an integral part of the Solar system, the Galaxy, and the Universe, about which space research is discovering more and more. This research yields many advantages for Earth itself, and it is therefore excellent that China announced at the G-20 summit, that it would share with developing countries the most advanced research results of its space and lunar exploration projects.

Mankind has arrived at a crossroads. If we continue to walk the well-trodden paths with the same old policies, the world will come apart. If, on the contrary, we can agree on the common aims of mankind—an economic and financial order that serves the well-being of all mankind, and which makes possible a decent life for every person on this Earth, the securing of raw materials and energy through higher technologies such as thermonuclear fusion, the exploration of space to safeguard our planet, and a renaissance of classical cultures—then we will be able to usher in a new, better era in the history of our species.

The General Assembly of the United Nations is the fitting place, where the new paradigm of our one mankind, based on that which comes before all the differences among nations, must be established and celebrated.

This statement has been translated from German.

REMOVE THE LIAR AND MURDERER BARACK OBAMA NOW!

The Cranes of Ibycus Are Here: The Moment for Justice Has Arrived!

by Robert Ingraham

Sept. 19—As this issue of the *Executive Intelligence Review* goes to press, a piece of legislation—the Justice Against Sponsors of Terrorism Act (JASTA)—sits on the desk of President Barack Obama, awaiting his action: to either sign it, or veto it and return it to Congress. He has until Sept. 23 to decide.

This bill, passed by the U.S. Senate in May of this year, and now passed unanimously by the House of Representatives on Sept. 9, would amend the Foreign Sovereign Immunities Act and the Anti-Terrorism Act, to allow federal civil lawsuits against the Kingdom of Saudi Arabia by the victims, families, and other injured parties from the Sept. 11, 2001 "9/11" attacks to proceed. Justice for these families and survivors will now be within reach, and the true authorship of the 9/11 attacks stands ready to be fully exposed.

The passage of JASTA was achieved only eight weeks after the release of the "28 Pages"—the previously classified section of the 2002 Report by the Senate Select Committee on Intelligence and the House Permanent Select Committee on Intelligence into the 9/11 attacks. Even within the partially redacted version of the "28 Pages" which was released, there is "incontrovertible evidence" that Saudi Arabian government officials were directly involved in financing and organizing the 9/11 attacks, and it has been precisely this evidence that both the Bush/Cheney administration and Barack Obama have been determined to hide from the American people over the past fifteen years.

It was mass murder. The truth was never told. Those responsible were never brought to justice. We have lived through fifteen years of lies. In the months and years since 9/11, many among us have abandoned all trust in the institutions of our Constitutional government. Many have given in to cynicism. Many have become afraid at the exercise of arbitrary government power. Many have become cowards.

But not everyone became cowardly, and through the efforts of handfuls of individuals in the U.S. Congress, among the survivors of 9/11, and within the LaRouche political movement, a powerful breakthrough has been accomplished. The mass murder of 3,000 American citizens on 9/11, and the subsequent fifteen years of lying by almost every top official of the Bush and Obama administrations—lying which has resulted in fifteen years of war, hundreds of thousands dead, millions displaced and unimaginable suffering—the truth of these matters is now all coming out, and the emergence of that truth, as the full implications become ever clearer, is enough for tens of millions of Americans to rise up in moral revulsion and justified anger and say: "Begone Obama. Not one more day. Not one more hour. Not one more minute. The lies, the deceit, the killings stop now."

The moment of reckoning has arrived.

I. "Look there! Look there, Timotheus! Behold the Cranes of Ibycus!"

Truth will out. Consider four developments that have taken place over the last two months:

1. July 6, 2016—Release of the Chilcot Report. On July 6, 2016, the Iraq Inquiry (also referred to as the Chilcot Inquiry after its chairman, Sir John Chilcot), a British public inquiry into that nation's role in the events leading up to the March, 2003 invasion of Iraq, released its final 6,000 page report, after seven years of hearings, investigations and testimony.

This report,[1] which has popularly become known as

---

1. The report can be found at: http://www.iraqinquiry.org.uk/

Photo by the U.S. Air Force

American war casualties returned to Dover AFB from Iraq in 2004.

the Chilcot Report, found:

• that there was no evidence that Saddam Hussein was involved in the 9/11 attacks;

• that Saddam Hussein did not pose any threat to British or American interests;

• that the intelligence presented regarding weapons of mass destruction was without merit (i.e., knowingly false);

• that the United Kingdom and United States had deliberately subverted the authority of the United Nations Security Council;

• that there was no legal basis for the 2003 invasion of Iraq.

The report revealed secret letters between British Prime Minister Tony Blair and George W. Bush revealing the role of Blair in manipulating and provoking the American President, including one where he says, "This is the moment when you can define international politics for the next generation: the true post-cold war world order."

There is no name-calling in the restrained language of the report, but the evidence of outright fraud and lying is explicit. After the release of the report, Tony

media/246416/the-report-of-the-iraq-inquiry_executive-summary.pdf

White House/Eric Draper

President George W. Bush meets with Saudi ambassador Prince Bandar bin Sultan at the Bush ranch in Crawford, Texas, Aug. 27, 2002.

Blair issued a statement "admitting mistakes" but simultaneously making an hysterical assertion that "there were no lies, there was no deceit." Reginald Keys, a founding member of Military Families Against the War, whose son was killed in Iraq in 2003, responded by calling Blair's statement the "ramblings of a madman."

With the release of the Chilcot Report, there is now no basis for a legitimate disagreement. The evidence has been compiled and presented. The Iraq War was based on lies, misinformation and the deliberate misleading of the people of Britain and the United States by the Bush/Cheney administration and British Prime Minister Tony Blair. Everything that has subsequently transpired in Iraq, Syria, Libya and elsewhere—all of the carnage and destruction—all stems from the lies that were told in 2003, lies which have continued to be told by the Obama Administration down to the present day.

2. July 15, 2016—Release of 28 Pages. In 2002, the Senate Select Committee on Intelligence and the House Permanent Select Committee on Intelligence issued the results of their Joint Inquiry, a 422 page Report into the terrorist attacks of Sept. 11, 2001. On orders from the Bush administration, 28 pages from that report were classified and withheld from the public. For the next seven years under George W. Bush, followed by seven more years under Barack Obama, the United States Presidency had refused to reveal the content of those 28 pages to the American people. Now, following a concerted fight by former U.S. Senator Bob Graham, Congressman Walter Jones, Congressman Stephen Lynch and others, the 28 Pages have been released.

What these pages show is the direct role of Saudi Arabia, including then Saudi Ambassador to the United States, Prince Bandar bin-Sultan, in financing the hi-

U.S. Navy Photo/Preston Keres

A New York City fireman calls for 10 more rescue workers to make their way into the rubble of the World Trade Center.

Saudi adviser to the nephew of King Fahd.

All of this evidence is now out and a matter of public record.

3. Sept. 9, 2016—Justice Against Sponsors of Terrorism Act (JASTA) Passed by House of Representatives. As stated above, this legislation will allow U.S. citizens the right to bring suits in federal court against the Kingdom of Saudi Arabia, Saudi officials, and others who were the true authors of the 9/11 attacks. At the same time, a prominent member of the British House of Commons has written recently in the *Daily Telegraph* that, under JASTA, the British Monarchy can be sued as well as the Saudis, because of London's longstanding support for the very same terrorists behind 9/11. The direct role of Britain in sponsoring the 9/11 attacks, as well as Barack Obama's continuing functioning as an agent of the British Crown, are now very much in the public spotlight.

Again, as in the release of the 28 Pages, this victory came through the personal courage of individual American citizens, including Terry Strada, the National Chair of 9/11 Families & Survivors United for Justice Against Terrorism. Mrs.

jackers of the planes which struck the World Trade Center on 9/11. The evidence of the Anglo-Saudi hand is overwhelming.[2]

Prince Bandar is himself a British agent. In 1985, he and Margaret Thatcher engineered the Al Yamamah oil-for-arms deal, through which the British and the Saudis amassed a secret, offshore slush fund in excess of $100 billion, to finance global terrorism, regime change and assassinations. Bandar, at the time of the 9/11 attacks, was so close to President George W. Bush that he was nicknamed "Bandar Bush." Leaked information from CIA and FBI documents alleges that Saudi government officials, including from the Saudi embassy in Washington and the consulate in Los Angeles, gave the hijackers both financial and logistical aid. Named were Prince Bandar, accredited Saudi diplomat Shaykh al-Thumairy, apparent Saudi intelligence agents Osama Bassnan and Omar al-Bayoumi, and Esam Ghazzawi, a

EIRNS/Alicia Cerretani

Congressman Walter Jones (R-NC), at a press conference to promote the House bill calling for the release of the 28 pages of the Congressional Joint Inquiry Report on 9/11, is joined here by 9/11 family members Terry, Justin, and Kaitlin Strada.

Strada has called for a protest outside the White House on Tuesday, Sept. 20 to demand that Obama either sign the bill into law or cast his veto to allow Congress to do its patriotic duty and override his shameful action.

On Monday, Sept. 12, White House Press Secretary Josh Earnest announced that U.S. President Barack Obama would likely veto the JASTA bill. On Sept. 15, Lyndon LaRouche commented that he expects Obama to veto JASTA, "because he is an agent of the British System."

If Obama takes that route, given that JASTA passed in both the House and Senate by unanimous voice votes, an override of the President's veto is likely. How-

---

2. The full text of the 28 Pages can be found at: https://28pages.org/the-declassified-28-pages/

ever, Obama's—and London's—opposition to the legislation is so fierce almost anything is possible, including a maneuver to recess Congress before they can take up a veto-override vote.

The release of the 28 Pages, together with the enactment of the JASTA bill, also open the door for investigating literally millions of pages of other government documents from the investigation into 9/11 that remain classified to this day. Sen. Bob Graham, Rep. Walter Jones and other leaders of the fight for the truth about 9/11 have demanded that the government release all of these secret files. As Graham told an audience at the National Press Club in Washington, the release of the 28 pages "popped the cork on the bottle, and now we must see the entire contents."

rt/youtube
The premeditated burning of the U.S. Mission in Benghazi, Libya on Sept. 11, 2012.

4. Sept. 13, 2016—Release of House of Commons Foreign Affairs Select Committee Report on War on Libya.[3] In what

some have characterized as "Chilcot 2," on Sept. 13 the Foreign Affairs Select Committee of the British House of Commons released its Report into the March, 2011 NATO actions which resulted in the murder of Libyan President Muammar Qaddafi and the destruction of the Libyan nation.

White House Photo by Lawrence Jackson
President Barack Obama, with Secretary of State Hillary Rodham Clinton, delivers a statement in the Rose Garden of the White House, Sept. 12, 2012, regarding the attack on the U.S. consulate in Benghazi, Libya.

The House of Commons Report is explicit—much like the Chilcot Report—that the U.S./British military intervention is Libya was based on faked intelligence, hidden motives, lies and half truths. From the beginning the aim was "regime change" in Libya. The Report excoriates the British Prime Minister David Cameron whom they name as "ultimately responsible" for everything that subsequently happened in Libya. One day prior to the release of the Report, Cameron was forced

to resign his seat in the British Parliament.

What the American news media have so far failed to report, is that although the "scathing" Libya report nails Cameron, it is even more precise in the evidence it presents regarding Barack Obama, naming him as the one actually responsible for the chaos that was unleashed in Libya, chaos that enabled ISIS to come into being, and handed Libya over to the very jihadists who both murdered U.S. Ambassador J. Christopher Stevens in Benghazi on Sept. 11, 2012, and initiated the transfer of huge amounts of Libyan arms to ISIS in both Syria and Iraq.

The Report states, "The United States was instrumental in extending the terms of Resolution 1973 beyond the imposition of a no-fly zone to include the authorization of all necessary measures to protect civilians. In practice, this led to the imposition of a no-drive zone and the assumed authority to attack the entire Libyan Government command and communications network." Lord William Hague, who was British Foreign Secretary in 2011, said in his testimony to the Committee that it was the Obama Administration that changed the UN resolution backed by Cameron and the

---

3. The report can be found at: http://www.publications.parliament.uk/pa/cm201617/cmselect/cmfaff/119/119.pdf

British from "no-fly zone" to "all necessary measures."

On April 14, 2011, the *New York Times* published a signed op-ed by Barack Obama, David Cameron, and French President Nicolas Sarkozy, in which the three of them said, "Qaddafi must go, and go for good." So, they—these three heads of state—were all lying openly; and if anything, Obama did more heavy lifting to create this disaster than either Sarkozy or Cameron. He was responsible for the major decisions, including a conscious decision to assassinate a foreign leader.

All of this, of course is also very bad news for Hillary Clinton, the then-U.S. Secretary of State, who has backed the Obama Libya policy to this day, and who personally lied to Congress by repeating the hoax that it was a YouTube video that led to the murder of Ambassador Stevens.

unwebtv.org

In comments to the media on Sept. 17, Samantha Power, Permanent Representative of the United States to the UN, attacked Russia's role in Syria after U.S. and Australian jets killed 62 Syrian troops in Deir es-Zar, Syria.

II. Why Is Obama Still President?

On Oct. 21, 2012, one year after the murder of Muammar Qaddafi, Lyndon LaRouche authored a statement titled, *Obama's Murder of Qaddafi Is Deadly Threat to World Peace,* wherein he states,

> The role of President Obama in the murder of Libya's Qaddafi, has promoted an implicitly deadly threat to world peace, one which is combined with the presently onrushing, general economic breakdown-crisis now raging throughout both Europe and the trans-Atlantic system. This arrangement presently represents a degree of qualitative threat greater than that which existed throughout the intervals of two preceding, so-called "World Wars."[4]

Now, four years after this prescient statement by LaRouche, and having lived through the ensuing destruction of Libya, the carnage in Syria, and the inhuman "refugee crisis" which has engulfed the Mediterranean region and all of western Europe, the accuracy of Mr. LaRouche's remarks is proven.

Why is Barack Obama still in office? Why do Amer-

icans believe anything that Obama says? He is a liar. He lies, and then he lies again, and then he lies again.

Former British Prime Minister David Cameron, Obama's partner in the crimes committed against Libya in 2011, has been forced to resign from Parliament. How does Obama escape for the same crimes? The same arms sales to terrorists? The same coverups? Everything that was proven about the conduct and actions of David Cameron was also proven as to Barack Obama. Why is he still President?

Syria

On Sept. 17, U.S. and Australian jets attacked Syrian troops at Deir ez-Zor in Syria, killing 62 Syrian soldiers, soldiers who were engaged in deadly combat against ISIS terrorists. When Russia responded by immediately convening an emergency meeting of the U.N. Security Council, U.S. Ambassador—and Obama intimate—Samantha Power accused the Russians of "grandstanding" and then proceeded to deny the accuracy of the report, only admitting that if such an attack were to be proven to have occurred, that it was, of course, the case that it was all an "accident" and that the United States "regretted" the loss of life.

The Russian Foreign Ministry spokeswoman Maria Zakharova, however, blasted the Obama administration in no uncertain terms, "After today's airstrikes on the Syrian army, we come to a really terrifying conclusion for the entire world: The White House is defending IS. Now there can be no doubts about that." Similarly, Russian U.N. Ambassador Vitaly Churkin responded to the situation, stating to the press:

---

4. The full statement can be found at: http://archive.larouchepac.com/node/24269

It is highly suspicious that the U.S. chose to conduct this particular airstrike at this time.... It was quite significant and not accidental that it happened just two days before the Russian-American arrangements were supposed to come into full force.

The Syrian Foreign Ministry statement was equally explicit:

This attack is deliberate, and the U.S. has plotted it in order to implement its strategy in continuing the terrorist war against the Syrian army ... [It] highlights the coordination between this terrorist organization [ISIS] and the United States.

Lyndon LaRouche was even more straightforward, emphasizing that Obama is clinically insane and is planning to launch warfare. He is crazy and a real threat, LaRouche stated, but I don't think he can pull it off. Obama always does these kinds of things: he commits an atrocity, and then tries to deny responsibility for it. The charges coming from Russian and Syrian authorities are important and constitute a challenge to Obama's intentions.

III. A Personal Decision to Act

So why is Obama still the President of the United States?

To answer that, I refer the reader to another article in this current issue of *Executive Intelligence Review*. During the Thursday, Sept. 15 LaRouche PAC National Fireside Chat, Manhattan Project leader Dennis Speed responded to a question on the subject of cowardice by saying:

The real point is, that there's a moral obligation on the part of the rest of us, *to stand against [evil], in a completely and utterly uncompromising way*. That *that's* the issue. Not the fact that the British or others, are capable of manipulating that evil against human beings, our point has to be: We reject the conception that human creativity on the part of each and every one of us does not carry an *obligation* to fight against evil. And for many people that's their first access to creativity, to say: I will fight against evil, and I will figure out how to defeat it.

If one looks at the successful fight that resulted in the passage of JASTA or the release of the 28 Pages, this was accomplished by the willingness of singular human beings to stand against evil. Lyndon LaRouche; members of the LaRouche PAC Policy Committee; leaders of the Manhattan Project; participants in the recent Living Memorial concerts of Mozart's *Requiem*; individual former and current members of Congress, most particularly Senator Graham and Congressman Walter Jones; leaders of the fight to secure the release of the 28 Pages such as Terry Strada, and many others—these are people of courage.

These are not millions. Their power is not in numbers, but in the moral courage to fight. There is no need to compile "evidence" against Obama. The individuals mentioned above have already done that. The evidence is in the Chilcot Report, the 28 Pages, the House of Commons Report on Libya. It's all already there.

All that is required is to recognize that merely *one day more* of the existence of the Presidency of Barack Obama, is one day more that the human race is held hostage to evil. If Obama actually vetoes the JASTA legislation, anyone—at that point—who does not act for his immediate removal is committing a crime against the nation and against all future generations.

The Breaking Point

On June 9, 1954, during a Congressional Committee meeting of the "Army-McCarthy" hearings, the U.S. Army's attorney Joseph N. Welch, in response to wild accusations by Senator Joseph McCarthy, challenged McCarthy, "Have you no sense of decency, sir, at long last?" That question, asked at that moment, not only silenced McCarthy; it also resonated with tens of millions of Americans, who since the death of Franklin Roosevelt had stood by silently in fear and cowardice, as their fellow citizens had been persecuted and the nation's mission perverted. The shame of tolerating evil, the shame of allowing one's own sense of decency to remain mute was made tangible.

This is all that is required today to remove Obama. Now. Today. Instantly. A personal refusal to tolerate the shame that comes from acquiescing to that which one knows to be evil. The absolute refusal to tolerate it any further.

Obama lies about everything: the drone killings, the economy, Glass-Steagall, China, Russia, the Ukraine, Syria, Libya, health care, 9/11, the Saudis. He lies about everything. And everyone knows it.

Have you no shame? Have you no decency? Act!

Every Day Counts In Today's Showdown To Save Civilization

That's why you need EIR's **Daily Alert Service**, a strategic overview compiled with the input of Lyndon LaRouche, and delivered to your email 5 days a week.

For example: On Jan. 7, EIR's Daily Alert featured the British hand behind the pattern of global provocations toward war. Of special note is British Intelligence's role in instigating the Saudi Kingdom's attempt to set off a Sunni-Shia war. This religious war has been the intent of British strategy since the Blair-Bush attack on Iraq in 2003.

We also uniquely update you regularly on the progress toward the release of the suppressed 28 pages of the Congressional Inquiry on 9/11, which would expose the Saudi role.

Every edition highlights the reality of the impending financial crash/bail-in policies that would realize the British goal of mass depopulation.

This is intelligence you need to act on, if we are going to survive as a nation and a species. Can you really afford to be without it?

THURSDAY, JANUARY 7, 2016

Volume 2, Number 97

EIR Daily Alert Service

P.O. BOX 17390, WASHINGTON, DC 20041-0390

- British Crown Pushing War and Genocide in 2016
- Financial Mudslide Goes On; Monetarist Tyranny Gloats over Bail-Ins
- Moody's Downgrades Portugal's Novo Banco
- Puerto Rico's Default: It's Every Vulture for Himself
- Wide Glass-Steagall Debate Set Off Again by Sanders Speech
- MI6 Mouthpiece Evans-Pritchard Touts Persian Gulf Chaos
- North Korea Tests a Miniaturized Hydrogen Bomb
- Uighur Terrorists Found in Indonesia
- Foreign Investors Are Flocking In to China

EDITORIAL

British Crown Pushing War and Genocide in 2016

✂

II. The Secret of Human Creativity

The Remedy for the Evil of Obama

The following edited excerpts are taken from the weekly LaRouche PAC National Fireside Chat of Sept. 15, 2016. The guest speaker was Dennis Speed, a leader of both the LaRouche PAC and the Manhattan Project.

Bill Roberts: Everyone should know that the JASTA bill passed unanimously out of the House last week, after earlier passing the Senate unanimously. Of course, this is something that 9/11 widow Terry Strada and many Congressmen have fought for over years, to have justice for the victims of 9/11, and their families and loved ones, by bringing the Saudi Kingdom to justice for their role in 9/11. As far as we know, Obama is still threatening to veto this, and we shouldn't be surprised if he tries some trick to push this back and defeat it. The only question should be: why have the American people tolerated this man, who is a murderer, and has protected the greatest mass murder of Americans in the history of the United States.

So, many of you have participated over the last weekend in the living memorial that was organized in New York City. Dennis may have more to say about this, but this was organized to address this very question, of

Percey B. Shelley

the cowardice in the American population, the capitulation to fear and evil, to allow people to break from that and make them conscious of how they've been behaving, and to establish a higher standard within them to recognize why they were allowing such behavior. I'm going to leave it at that, and ask if Dennis would like to say something at this point, or go directly to questions.

Dennis Speed: I want to say something about the change that has occurred as a result of the last week. Lyndon LaRouche is the most important living thinker

of our time. Of course, all great thinkers never die, but Lyn happens to be here with us in the flesh and is able to inspire people to forms of creativity they did not know were possible. This is important to understand, and it is important to think about.

Now, there's one particular matter I'd like to bring to people's attention. From at least 1973, and actually before that time, LaRouche expressed, in various written forms, his love of and appreciation for the ideas of Percy Shelley's *A Defence of Poetry,* and I'd like to refer at the beginning of our discussion, to the first paragraph of that writing by Percy Shelley. Often we refer to it, and we talk about the idea of man having profound and impassioned conceptions respecting man and nature—conceptions that at certain periods of time are able to be received and imparted at an extraordinary rate. In other words, things that people could not learn for decades, they can literally learn in days or weeks. But the thing that distinguishes Lyn, and what he's done, is that he's dedicated his life to the idea of providing the means by which the individual can focus on the idea of creativity, that which distinguishes man from beast, and can access directly his individual or her individual creativity and *change the world.*

Now, this isn't done by some act of individual, arbitrary will. It isn't done in the ways that people normally think *at all,* and I think Lyn is the best one to express the fact that his notion of human identity is not at all the same idea as that which most people have of what is human. The human identity is not biological. What Einstein represents as a thinker, and I think in a different way what Shelley represented as a thinker, is what Lyn often refers to.

And I only wanted to refer to one element of what Shelley is talking about. He's speaking here about the difference between reason and imagination. And he says:

> According to one mode of regarding those two classes of mental action which are called reason and imagination, the former may be considered as mind contemplating the relations borne by one thought to another, however produced; and the latter, as mind acting upon those thoughts so as to color them with its own light, and composing from them, as from elements, other thoughts, each containing within itself the principle of its own integrity.

That is, imagination is a compositional process of the highest order. When we speak about music, for example, this is the concept that the Mozart *Requiem* and the *Requiem* performances that John Sigerson conducted, I think, attempted to convey. That we are capable of inventing something new, and that musical composition is a case of that, that the work—the *Requiem* in this particular case, of Mozart—or the works of Bach, or others, invent something never before seen in the Universe.

They are not recombinations of earlier thoughts. They are not recombinations of earlier physical principles. It's an introduction as a *completely new principle, using the imagination.* And when that is done, the thing that is done, by introducing *this* kind of imaginative, creative principle, cannot die. It is immortal. And it is the way in which mankind accesses the principle of immortality which characterizes the Universe itself and the being of the Universe or the Composer of the Universe.

Now, I think what's important about stating that, and that's the best I can state it;—Lyn would have I think a better conception of that,—but the reason for saying this is that it is from *this* standpoint that the only efficient method of strategy comes. A discussion about anything lower than that is actually not human, and that matters such as issues, the kind of issues that we tend to be plagued by in the so-called political campaigns *are not human.* Many of the statements of the kinds of things that people talk about, however validating they seem to be in themselves, *are not human statements.*

If we start talking about things like police brutality, for example, or the way that most people discuss poverty, for example, or the way that most people discuss other so-called human needs, it is not a *human way* of discussing it. You're discussing these things *devoid* of the imaginative or creative principle, which can be brought to bear as a strategic idea.

Now, what the Chinese have been doing, what Vladimir Putin has been doing, *these ways* of approaching the idea of strategy, which are congruent with the way in which LaRouche has approached strategy his entire life, *this* gives us a *human* economics, a *human* politics. This is to be contrasted with what we presently have coming from Obama, Hillary Clinton, Donald Trump, and much of what we see through the rest of the world as a whole.

So the intent of what we did with our musical performances was to raise the standard in the United States, raise, if you will, the guidon of reason of humanity, and so, these were not musical performances. This was a form of creative intervention, which was intended to allow, or to set the stage for further development or advancement of the outlook that was expressed, for example, by Vladimir Putin last year at the United Nations, or at the G-20 Summit that the Chinese just hosted at Hangzhou. This is what we're doing. This is our approach. This is the way we have, if you will, attempted to reorient political life in the United States. And it's the beginning of a set of actions that we will be taking in the future.

So I just wanted to say that, and now we should open up and go to any questions or any statements that people have. And we'll do our best to answer the questions.

What is the Manhattan Project?

Question: Hi, this A—, here in New York. What I wanted to raise to you, Dennis, is running parallel to the building for the audience for the past two weeks or so, where we know that upwards of easily 10,000 leaflets were distributed in New York, with a distribution of the broadsheet, which had also picked up in its massive distribution. So here are two seemingly on one hand parallel operations taking place, yet we have this tremendous turnout and effect in New York.

Can you talk with us about how these two elements are really the same thing, and as well as, where do we go now? With the UN in town, with all the overview that was just provided us, what's our next move forward, lest we rest on what we accomplished this weekend?

Speed: Well, let me just say this. The first thing to remember is that the process that's under way in New York is the Manhattan Project. Lyndon LaRouche created this in the fall of 2014. He saw the initiative and saw the potential, and urged us to work with him, and in the first phases of that work, much of it was not *ignoring* what he said, making sure that you would go back

Library of Congress

Hamilton's home—Grange—in upper Manhattan, was completed two years before he was murdered.

to the drawing board. You thought you were doing the right thing, you would come back, he would give different advice about it, and what happened with that, as we began to do that, it became rather natural for him, for LaRouche directly, to initiate a process of dialogue with a group of people in New York.

Now, this was his way of resurrecting Alexander Hamilton's idea of the Presidency of the United States. He recognized that it was necessary to have a Presidential orientation and that there was no President available. And that Obama has to be removed from office, but that the American people had largely, through a failure of nerve and other problems, walked away from this task.

So, Lyn created the dialogue process. The dialogue process led in various ways, for various people to work with LaRouche, and then the various things that happened, whether that be the broadsheet or other matters, were the natural capabilities that became available.

Now, I don't want to be too sequential, because in one sense that's too formal. The truth of the matter is, that we're in a situation where the United States needs a future. LaRouche has provided the conception of the United States's future for decades, but, specifically, and in the context of the Obama Presidency, it became urgently necessary that the fact that Obama must not be President of the United States *a single day more,* must be emphasized, and *re*-emphasized. Despite the fact that people, out of despair or cowardice would believe the opposite.

So if you look at what's now just happened: You've had in July the 28 pages being released; you had the Sept. 9th passage of JASTA, the Justice Against Sponsors of Terrorism Act; and now you have had many other things that have begun to happen. And now, of course, the prospect or the possibility of Obama's impeachment is being brought to us by Obama himself.

Now the important thing here is to recognize that what LaRouche was saying was possible, and people believed to be *impossible,* from basically April of 2009, now becomes manifest in its own way, as being the natural course of things! So how come he knew this, when other people didn't know it? This is what we mean by *human* politics, or the human principle of creativity.

So I would just put it that way, and the issue is not falling back, the issue is different. The issue is people should simply recognize that this had been something that LaRouche said we're going to do, said could be done, and we're now sitting there with the evidence, if you want to put it that way, of the truth of that principle, and it's just a matter of activating other American citizens to take advantage of that fact. That's what I would say.

Question: Hi Dennis, this is R— out in Oregon. I'm trying to think about all of this while you're giving the briefing. I wonder, I'm just musing to myself, is Obama in check or checkmate? Because if he signed JASTA, he's admitting that he's covered up Saudi complicity for the last eight years. And if he refuses to sign, he's standing down and thumbing his nose at the entire delegation of the Congress of the United States assembled. And neither one of those looks like a promising option for him.

But could you reiterate perhaps, what you opened with, and maybe say something else about Shelley and the creative principle in this situation?

Speed: Well let's just get the thing with Obama straight. Remember that Obama is never checked, because Obama is not deploying as a human being. Obama is deploying as the agent of the British Empire. Now, what has happened is that we have created a certain kind of trap, and since he acts from a bestial standpoint—he has a bestial identity—he behaves like a beast. So he's in, in that sense, a position to be taken down, but that's not going to happen unless the American people act. For example, you can not act through the electoral process presently. You can do things, you can address the issue of Obama through the electoral process, in some respects. Not through Trump or through Hillary, but through the process that we're conducting. So let's take, for example, the issue of JASTA or some of these other things. It's not that these issues in themselves bring Obama down. It's simply that his

EIRNW/Stuart Lewis

Violinist Norbert Brainin, a founder of the Amadeus Quartet.

EIRNS/Philip Ulanowsky

Manhattan Project scientist Dr. Robert Moon leads a science class with young students in July 1986.

EIRNS/Stuart Lewis

Lyndon LaRouche greets Marie Madeleine Fourcade, a leader in the World War II French resistance networks, at the founding conference of the U.S. affiliate of the Schiller Institute on July 3, 1984.

nature is revealed. The nature of the British operation that spawned him, controls him, and deploys him. That's what has happened.

So Obama is not going to give in. Obama is not going to somehow relent. Obama's not going to somehow, say to us, "Oh yeah, you're right. I've got to act like a human being." That isn't going to happen. But what is true is that we've done our job and gotten the country to a certain point, and ...

Let's just be straightforward: Many of the people who have often been on the phone calls, are no longer really on these phone calls in the same way, because they were either angry, or frustrated by the idea that, when they would ask us to endorse Donald Trump, for example, or other such things, we would say "no." We would say, "No, because he isn't human." And then they would get mad, because "Well, you say I'm not

EIRNS

Guyana Foreign Affairs Minister and Justice Minister, Fred Wills, addressing the UN General Assembly on Sept. 8, 1976. He said that the time had come for a debt moratorium for the developing sector.

EIRNS

Scientist and philosopher Pobisk G. Kuznetsov, left, with Lyndon LaRouche, in Russia, April 1994.

voting for a human being, that kind of insults me." Well, but the problem involved is that *Donald Trump doesn't really exist*, just like Obama doesn't really exist. You're not dealing with anything human. It doesn't mean that Trump might not say something correct at some point. Or someone else may say it. But the issue of *Obama* is *the British Imperial system* and the destruction of what that represents: It's not human.

Now, what Shelley represented and why Lyn emphasized this very, very early—and he's always emphasized this. If you look at the people Lyn has worked with in politics, and in other fields, they're always people who distinguish themselves in whatever field as being *creative, imaginative minds.* And so whether we're talking about the violinist Norbert Brainin, the scientist Robert Moon, or we're talking about the French Resistance fighter Marie-Madeleine Fourcade, or we're talking about Hulan Jack, the former Borough President of Manhattan, or Fred Wills, the former Foreign Minister of Guyana,—there are many different people we could cite; the economists, like Taras Muranivsky in Russia; or scientist Pobisk Kuznetsov from Russia; whoever it is that LaRouche has been close to, has distinguished themselves as a fundamentally creative mind, that stand above the practices and actions of many other people in their fields.

What's the issue? If you want a President of the United States, a Hamiltonian President of the United States, a President like a Franklin Roosevelt, it's got to be that you activate the principle of creativity, and you lead the American people from that standpoint. This doesn't mean you're necessarily popular. But it means you're correct, you're right, and people recognize that, and they'll follow that.

So the issue of Obama—no Obama's not in check. That's obvious: He's still there. If Obama were in check, he wouldn't be in office. So, no, he's not in check. The point of the thing is that if the American people are willing to dispose of the vampire-like Barack Obama, who is deployed on behalf of a principle of evil, then he can be removed from office. But if you're terrified of the vampire, and you refuse to take the necessary measures, which people all know about, of how you get rid of vampires, then he will continue to do what *his nature* causes him to do. So this is the important thing to understand: It's *his nature* for Barack Obama to do what he's doing. You are not going to change that, because he has no inclination to act in a human fashion.

So he's not in check! And every day that goes by that he is still in the Presidency, the entire world is threatened. What happened with Cameron, indicates what *could* happen with Obama, at any moment, were the American people mobilized behind what Lyn is saying. So I think that's the important thing to understand. And you *cannot do* that, by merely attempting to quote/unquote "vote for the lesser of two evils," be that Trump or Hillary,— and there is where the cowardice of a lot of people, including even people in our own networks, continues to be manifest. We tried to address that with the concerts, and I think we did the best we could.

cc/Elizabeth Cromwell

President Obama's policies have been purveyors of cultural despair.

What is Creativity?

Question: Hello, this is L— from Michigan. I'd say it's a pretty big story, David Cameron resigning or getting impeached in the British Parliament or whatever, and I didn't read it anywhere else, except reading it on LaRouche PAC site. How did that happen, how did they come to that conclusion? And what type of evidence is compiled, or can be compiled against Obama, and how's it going to get to all the people, because we're not going to be hearing it on the media or the news or radio or anything like that. Where's the evidence compiled? You know, credible evidence compiled for the impeachment? I know that LaRouche PAC has quite a bit of evidence, but it doesn't seem like it's official. Who's going to compile the evidence and bring this, and get the people to understand that this is serious stuff? That these are impeachable crimes? That this is treason being committed by our elected officials?

Speed: The evidence for Barack Obama's impeachment is his existence. Now this is not a problem, and despair is not necessary. *We don't have to compile anything!* Let me explain why that's true: First of all, Terry Strada and the families of 9/11 have placed, through various assistance that we and others gave,— Walter Jones, Senator Graham, many other people,— we placed the matter of 9/11, and therefore Benghazi and many other crimes committed after 9/11, squarely in front of the American people. And for example, in the same way that once the Congress decided that it would tell Obama that it would no longer *appeal* to him to get the 28 pages, but they would simply take the prerogative of congressional action on behalf of the American people, and if necessary read the contents or express the content, on the floor of the Congress *without* Barack Obama, at *that* point the 28 pages got released!

Now, it wasn't quite so simple as I just said, but in other words, whereas for years, the supposed assumption was "well, we've got to somehow appeal to the

EIR Special Report

Obama's War on America: 9/11 Two

The Real Story Behind Benghazi

EIR Special Report

Obama's War on America: 9/11 Two

February 2013

Price **$100** (Paperback or PDF. For paper, add shipping and handling; Va. residents add 5% sales tax)

Order from **EIR News Service** 1-800-278-3135
Or online: **store.larouchepub.com**

President, and if the President deigns to do it, maybe we'll get the pages from him." But that wasn't the case. It was *cowardice* that was stopping the pages from being released, and a procedure was not required—what was required was to have the courage, and then the procedure, shall we say, would suddenly appear.

So this issue of "we have to compile the evidence as to why Obama has to be impeached"—No we don't! Everybody in America knows that Obama should be impeached. But they don't have the *guts* to do it. And that's why people keep running behind one or the other of these candidates and saying, "that's my responsibility as an American, I've got to vote; I'll vote for the lesser of two evils." But that's cowardice: Because the truth of the matter, first of all, is neither of those candidates may even *exist* on Election Day to be voted for! We don't know whether Hillary Clinton is going to get through this. We don't know whether Donald Trump will get through this. That's the truth! But one thing we *do* know, is that Barack Obama is still there!

So the issue for us is that we're in a position, right now, to remove Barack Obama. We don't have to do *anything* other than *insist that it must be done,* and we do that by two means: One, take things we've already developed in advance—take what we're doing, for example, on Glass-Steagall. That's in front of both Houses of Congress right now. We have, of course, JASTA. And it's been made clear, if he tries to go to a veto of that, well, does that show the American people? If the *entire Congress* has stated that those Saudis or others should be, in fact, held accountable; if Obama tries to stand up against *that* unanimous will of the American people, how can anyone deny, or doubt, that he clearly stands on the side of the *treason* against the United States?

So there's no *need* for us to do the various things that people are claiming they need to do! No! What is needed is, the courage to act in the way LaRouche has insisted ever since April of 2009, and *insist* that he be removed from office.

Question: Hello, Dennis, this is C— from California. My question is the nature of evil and also that the cowardice that you're talking about, is that the empire— people just are not born evil. They are made evil. One of the ways that it's done is to come through the cultural environment, but also through television and the whole culture we have, people— literally what they *see* is not a world that they think that they can deal with, and then they take various avoidances—as you say, cowardice. But it's not that the individual person, it's not an individual thing. It's actually a psychological manipulation. And people don't remember Trist and these guys; the guy coming out of World War I, that they devoted a science of controlling, let us say, the visual—when I say the visual I mean, what people see; they don't *see* the future. They can only see what's there. Can you comment on that?

Speed: OK. Well, yes, there is something called the Tavistock Institute for Human Relations, and yes, they're the brainwashing process. But the way Lyn talked about this, and had us illustrate it, now maybe twenty-two years ago, was in a thing called "The Palmerston Zoo." We gave a panel at one of the conferences, a group of us. And we tried to described how Lord Palmerston had designed—using ideological studies—the way in which the various elements of humanity in various areas of the world were self-controlled by ideology, by poisonous ideology which people refused to liberate themselves from.

One of the reasons why Lyndon LaRouche has often emphasized the figure of Moses Mendelssohn in the case of Germany, is that Moses Mendelssohn,—of course very poor, and Jewish, and limited in various ways,—he was from the ghetto—assimilated the highest levels of culture, of German culture, but also of other cultures, and became the exemplar, together with Lessing in their joint work with others like Kästner, and others, of what would become the actual modern, European Classical music tradition. It was through the work of Mendelssohn and Lessing, and Kästner and others that Bach, for example, was preserved, creating the essential ability to get to Mozart the knowledge of Bach. The knowledge and the rebirth of the focus on Bach, which came through the Mendelssohn family itself, and Felix Mendelssohn in particular, through his 1829 resurrection of the *St. Matthew Passion.*

Now, I'm citing that merely before I'm about to then

oil portrait (1771) by Anton Graff, University of Leipzig collection
Moses Mendelssohn (1729-1786) played an exemplary role in creating the modern European Classical music tradition.

hit you with the other element, which is,— yeah, people are not born evil. But here's the problem: Everyone has a responsibility, individually, as to whether or not they *accept* being evil! And so, yeah, you may not be born that way, but to *simply* claim that people are manipulated into being evil—No. No! That's the whole issue, actually, of the nature of evil in the world.

The individual free will,— and this is true for Barack Obama just as it's true for everybody else,— allows you to make a choice as to whether or not that becomes your identity. In the case of Barack Obama you're dealing with something which may not be pure evil, but it is *impure* evil. It's like saying, "well, Dracula is not born evil." Well,— but Dracula is a vampire, he's undead! So, Barack Obama—we're talking about the living dead, the undead! So, yes, you're correct that he was perhaps not born evil, but he's something which is unborn.

We're not talking about the simple question of his mother, and the things we said before; that was also highly unfortunate. And yes, people get very nervous when you say these kinds of things, for other reasons which I don't find valid around Barack Obama. But I think what's important, is to recognize that we wouldn't be concerned about him if he didn't hold office, that is, any office, ever, if he had not held office.

But he did. And so, we have to recognize that the problem of *one day more* of the existence of the so-called Presidency of Barack Obama, is one day more that the human race is held hostage to evil!

So, the real point is, that there's a moral obligation on the part of the rest of us, *to stand against that, in a completely and utterly uncompromising way. That's* the issue. Not the fact that the British or others are capable of manipulating that evil against human beings. Our point has to be: We reject the conception that human creativity on the part of each and every one of us does not carry an *obligation* to fight against evil. And for many people that's their first access to creativity, to say: I will fight against evil, and I will figure out how to defeat it.

No Future on the Frontiers of Science Unless We Dump the Subversive FBI

by Brian Lantz

Sept. 17—The FBI is an enemy of creativity. The FBI—the investigative arm of the Department of Justice—has, for example, shown again and again its hostility to American advances in science and technology. It attempted to strip Albert Einstein of his American citizenship. It attempted to frame the very competent NASA Administrator James Beggs and succeeded in forcing his resignation, with disastrous results. It went after Lyndon LaRouche in the 1980s to put an end to the Strategic Defense Initiative involving U.S.-Soviet cooperation to implement new physical principles for mutual security. LaRouche went to prison.

In 1999, Taiwanese-American scientist Wen Ho Lee at Los Alamos National Laboratory was indicted on charges of spying. After nine months in solitary confinement, he was convicted of nothing more than "improper handling of restricted data." In 2013, Chinese-Americans Guoqing Cao and Shuyu Li were accused of corporate espionage while employed at drug maker Eli Lilly and called "traitors." The charges were dropped in 2014. Xiaoxing Xi, chairman of the Physics Department of Temple University, and his family, were arrested by the FBI at gunpoint in their home in 2015. He was charged with having

NASA

The competent NASA administrator James M. Beggs was forced to resign in December 1985, when the FBI tried to frame him. One month later the shuttle Challenger exploded.

from Wen Ho Lee defense page

Taiwanese-American scientist Wen Ho Lee at the Los Alamos National Laboratory was indicted for spying in 1999, and held in solitary confinement for nine months. The government's case collapsed and he was convicted only of improper handling of sensitive data.

sent restricted American technology to China. Months later, all charges were withdrawn.

No scientist worth his or her salt could ignore such a string of seemingly anomalous actions for the sake of maintaining a naïve view of the FBI.

Who Owns the FBI?

As *EIR* has documented, the FBI was indeed *created* to accomplish the destruction of the United States as a sovereign nation.[1]

Lyndon LaRouche emphasizes that the roots of the FBI's methods lie in the 1901 assassination of President William McKinley—which led to Anglophile presidents such as Theodore Roosevelt and Woodrow Wilson—and Bertrand Russell's and mathematician David Hilbert's worldwide attack on the scientific outlook, beginning in 1900.

The creation of J. Edgar Hoover's FBI and its methods centers on Ralph Van Deman, known as the "father of American military intelligence," who was guided by his very experienced friend, Claude Dansey, of

---

1. The most recent such article is by Barbara Boyd, "Is the FBI Running You? Are You Sure?" *EIR*, Aug. 21, 2015, pp. 7-14.

British intelligence. Van Deman was, in turn, Hoover's mentor and remained one of his closest confidants until his death in 1952.

Van Deman modeled his methods directly on those of British intelligence, using what can loosely be termed "divide and rule" to "neutralize" revolutionary leaders and movements. Crudely utilizing those methods in the Philippines, Deman then went to British colonial India to gain further, first-hand experience. In the United States, in coordination with Hoover and Army Intelligence, he ran countless private citizen and vigilante operations to target "subversives," which were complemented by the power of the FBI and similar agencies on the state level.

Appropriately, Hoover was made an honorary Knight of the Order of the British Empire by King George VI in 1950.

Heinrich Himmler (left) and Adolf Hitler review SS troops during Reich Party Convention ceremonies.

Albert Einstein the 'Communist'

The FBI targeted Einstein in 1932 when he was offered a half-year appointment at the Institute for Advanced Study in Princeton, N.J. The operation to deny visas to Einstein and his wife Elsa involved one of Van Deman's cloned vigilante groups, the Women's Patriot Corporation, and elements of the U.S. State Department. The former labeled him "a Communist and menace to American institutions." Einstein used his immense prestige by going directly to the press and embarrassed the State Department into issuing their visas. When Hitler came to power early in 1933, the Nazis ransacked Einstein's Berlin apartment and declared him an enemy of the state. Einstein settled in the United States. But Einstein had an ongoing battle with Hoover and the FBI—waged with his notable and very effective genius—which continued until Einstein's death in 1955.[2]

During World War II, Einstein was quietly barred from the Manhattan Project—Army Intelligence did not want the American people to know. During the Truman/McCarthy "red scares," Einstein encouraged the scientific community and the American people to resist. In a letter of advice to William Frauenglass, a targeted high school English teacher in Brooklyn—

which Einstein and Frauenglass later jointly submitted to the *New York Times*—Einstein wrote:

> Reactionary politicians have managed to instill suspicion of all intellectual efforts into the public by dangling before their eyes a danger from without. Having succeeded so far, they are now proceeding to suppress the freedom of teaching and deprive of their positions all those who do not prove submissive, i.e., to starve them out.

Einstein's letter, which reveals the moral strength of character required of great scientists, calls upon his fellow intellectuals to act in "the revolutionary way of non-cooperation in the sense of Gandhi's. Every intellectual who is called before the committees ought to refuse to testify, i.e., must be prepared for jail and economic ruin, in short, for the sacrifice of his personal welfare in the interest of the cultural welfare of this country."

The letter appeared on the front page, on June 12, 1953.

Hoover was at that time attempting to build a case for stripping Einstein of his American citizenship! Hoover also feared that word of his efforts would leak out. Einstein knew his house was bugged—and it was—and that his friends and associates were being interviewed and otherwise intimidated. Should we be surprised that the Nazi leader, Heinrich Himmler, was on Hoover's "special correspondents" list until 1939?

---

2. The FBI files on Einstein, or rather, that part of the FBI files which the FBI is willing to acknowledge, have been released with many redactions under the Freedom of Information Act and are found at https://vault.fbi.gov/Albert%20Einstein

What is the meaning of the FBI operations against Albert Einstein? Was it any different than the Nazis' targeting of German scientist Max Planck, Einstein's collaborator and good friend? To some extent this article has already answered the question, but not satisfactorily. Why were the FBI *and* the Bertrand Russell networks deployed against Einstein? To answer that question, we must more firmly live and act *from the future*. Jason Ross of LaRouche's science team wrote, in a recent article:

> This great genius of the last century is the more remarkable for what followed him, or rather what failed to follow him. Within the shift in thinking at the turn of the twentieth century, especially towards mathematics and away from reality, both in physics and culturally—in essence, a rejection of mind as a component of the universe—Einstein stands out as a courageous pioneer demonstrating precisely that power of mind. His work ushered in a total reappraisal of the most basic concepts of science: those of space, time, energy and matter, and he continues to inspire new experiments offering new potentials for discovery, e.g., the construction and successful application of the LIGO project to detect gravitational waves. Why has the world not seen his equal since?

> Reached for comment today on Einstein's present-day importance, Lyndon LaRouche responded that the focus must be on developing mankind's power to discover his own nature, via children who go beyond their parents. That process, that rate of fostering creativity in future generations, is a measure of development. He concluded, "It's not Einstein's mathematics; it's the self-creation of the human species. *That* defines the nature of the human individual."

Be like Einstein: be a *mensch*.

Qian's Case: Is Brilliance Subversive?

In 1935 Qian Xuesen (sometimes transliterated Tsien Hsue-shen), then a 24-year-old mainland Chinese student, used a scholarship to get to M.I.T. and then to Caltech to earn his doctorate. Theodore von Kármán, the legendary Hungarian-American aerodynamicist, pronounced Qian an "undisputed genius" and made him one of his closest collaborators. In No-

Qian Xuesen, one of the founders of the Jet Propulsion Laboratory at Caltech, was targetted by Joe McCarthy's red scare and was deported. He had been a colonel in the U.S. Army. He became the father of China's rocket program.

vember 1943, Qian was one of the founders with von Kármán of the Jet Propulsion Laboratory at Caltech, which has played a vital role in the U.S. space program. During World War II, Qian contributed groundbreaking work on ballistics. Made a Colonel in the U.S. Army, Qian was among those who debriefed the German rocket scientists at Peenemünde at the end of the war.

Because of his important scientific role, Qian was targeted in the "Second Red Scare" (1950-57) run by the notorious Joe McCarthy with Hoover's side-kick, Roy Cohn, at his side. The FBI accused him of being a Communist sympathizer and of attempting to steal secret documents. Subsequent examination of the documents showed they contained no classified material. Although allowed to continue teaching at Caltech, he was effectively subjected to five years of house arrest. He was never prosecuted. In 1955 he was finally deported; by that time he was eager to return to China, where his brilliance was appreciated. A pre-eminent scientist in several fields, Qian went on to lead the People's Republic of China's ballistic missile and space programs and died in 2009 at age 97. He had also had a role in its nuclear weapons program.

After his return to China, former Navy Secretary Dan Kimball, who knew him personally, said, "He was no more a Communist than I was, and we forced him to go." In 1987, Dr. Qian was awarded Caltech's distinguished Alumni Award for his lifetime achievements.

The FBI Assault on NASA

NASA Administrator James Beggs was indicted in 1985 for allegedly violating federal procurement regulations years earlier, when he had been executive vice president at General Dynamics. Although a very competent head of NASA, he was forced to take an indefinite leave of absence.

One month after his resignation, with NASA under the incompetent Acting Administrator William Graham, Space Shuttle orbiter Challenger was launched from Kennedy Space Center in freezing weather, weather too cold for a safe launch. The ship exploded, killing seven of our precious astronauts. There had been controversy in NASA that morning over whether to launch. Beggs, who still maintained an office, was in his office and said it was too cold. But Graham approved the launch.

The story behind the story is bigger than the FBI, as usual. Graham, an outsider to NASA, had been sworn in as its Deputy Administrator in November 1985, apparently in anticipation of the indictment of Beggs in December. His previous experience was in weapons research. As Acting Administrator, he had made clear his intention to clear out the senior, most experienced people leading NASA. Not only was that leadership highly competent technically, much of it also had a very infectious technological optimism. Beggs himself had attacked the Club of Rome and Malthusians generally in a 1984 speech. The Challenger disaster damaged Graham's ability to carry out his plans, and he left NASA in October 1986 to become the director of the White House Office of Science and Technology Policy.

All charges against Beggs and his co-defendants were dropped in 1987. At a press conference, Beggs said that the charges had been politically motivated. He

FBI Agent James Hal Francis, operating under the name John Clifford, carried out an operation—Operation Lightning Strike—at the Johnson Space Center in Houston in an attempt to induce criminal acts.

received a belated letter of apology from Attorney General Edwin Meese in 1988 as Meese was leaving office, after one of his deputies, for a year, had refused to apologize.[3]

In the same decade, the FBI also mounted extensive operations against Lyndon LaRouche, the author of President Ronald Reagan's Strategic Defense Initiative (SDI), premised on international scientific cooperation with the Soviet Union in developing defensive systems based on new physical principles that would render thermonuclear weapons obsolete. LaRouche was also, naturally, an outspoken and influential advocate for the U.S. Space Program. And LaRouche defended Beggs.

Scientific progress depends on cooperation and collaboration, including on the international level. It is, in fact, *mission critical*, but the FBI consistently opposes it.

'Despicable, Disgusting, Rotten'

In 1991 the FBI again targeted NASA's manned space program, headquartered at Johnson Space Center in Houston, this time with an operation code-named Operation Lightning Strike, directed and coordinated from FBI headquarters. Special Agent James "Hal" Francis was deployed to Houston as "John Clifford" to carry out a fishing expedition. He set up a phony company, complete with a financial history and ratings. The intention was not to entrap a known criminal; there was *no evidence* that anyone at Johnson Space Center was doing anything illegal. The purpose was to induce criminal acts.

"John Clifford" was peddling a miniaturized lithotripter, a device that uses ultrasound to break up kidney stones and gall stones. This one was a fake, created for the FBI by a real, existing company. Its apparent merit was its small size—it was small enough to be used on the Space Shuttle. Higher-ups at FBI headquarters oversaw the targeting, starting at the top of NASA's

<hr />

3. For more on Beggs and the attack on NASA, see Marsha Freeman, "How the Space Shuttle Program Was Sabotaged," *EIR*, March 28, 1986, pp. 48-57 and 72.

manned space program. Targets included the then head of the Life Sciences Division, and former NASA Administrator James Beggs and his Washington consulting firm. They were approached to "influence-peddle" the fake lithotripter to NASA headquarters and in Congress. The FBI's scam did not work.

Astronaut David Wolf, another target in the sting, appeared on the NBC Nightly News and revealed that Clifford/Francis had telephoned him nearly twenty times to try to get him to accept a favor in exchange for influence peddling. Astronauts are American heroes, and the FBI had been desperate to change that. Along with NASA professionals and good, hardworking "ma and pa shop" NASA contractors, it was the American public that was dragged through this filth.

The FBI's Lightning Strike unearthed *no prior criminal activity*. In the end, only small fish—two lower level NASA employees and seven contractors—were entrapped, and then psychologically worked over and induced to plead guilty to lesser charges, or induced to implicate others to avoid further prosecution. Only one defendant, Dale Brown, fought the charges in court— and he won. Lives and careers were ruined. There was also serious damage to the functioning of NASA.

In 1994, after Operation Lightning Strike had (at least officially) ended, James Beggs explained to *Houston Press* reporter Steve McVickers what that damage was, and what he thought of the FBI's intentions:

> I think the whole idea of the government running stings in which you [use] government employees who lie and offer bribes with impunity, I think that's outrageous. I don't see any difference in that from what the Nazis did. *What* really *disturbs me about them doing this kind of thing to NASA is that you sow the seeds of distrust among the people in the agency who are responsible for running a very difficult and exceedingly hazardous program. To sow the seeds of distrust, deliberately, in that program is about as despicable and disgusting and rotten a thing to do as I can imagine.* [Emphasis added.][4]

FBI operations aim at destroying *collaboration*. Re-

flect on what is actually being organized by the leading nations of mankind—with the current, unfortunate exception of our United States. Particularly the New Silk Road initiatives and the results of the G-20 Summit in Hangzhou, China, Sept. 4-5, premised, as they are, on building mutual respect and collaboration among nations.[5] That is what's now in the air! Why then tolerate these dirty, secret police operations, intertwined as they are with cynical geopolitics, that sow mistrust and undermine the work and the lives of our scientists and scientific organizations, and mankind's greatest endeavors. After all, what is man really?

FBI Terror Against Chinese-Americans Today

Recall the more recent cases mentioned at the beginning. Taiwanese-American scientist Wen Ho Lee, working at a U.S. national laboratory in 1999, is indicted for spying, *spends nine months in solitary confinement*, and is convicted of nothing more than mishandling restricted data.[6] Chinese-Americans Guoqing Cao and Shuyu Li are accused of corporate espionage in 2013 and *are called "traitors"* by the prosecution. The charges are dropped. Xiaoxing Xi, chairman of the Physics Department of Temple University, and his family, *are arrested at gunpoint* by the FBI in their home in 2015. He is charged with having sent restricted technology to China. Months later all charges are withdrawn, but without prejudice to possibly charging him again. Meanwhile, free-wheeling claims of "Chinese hackers" are also being used to intimidate Chinese-American high-tech companies.

In a June 2016 town meeting in his district, Texas Congressman John Culberson (R), whose Appropriations subcommittee controls funds for both the FBI and NASA, raved, "You don't know how many closed door meetings I've had with the FBI about the Chinese." "The Chinese steal everything," he said. This, then, is Culberson's report: The un-American activities at the FBI are alive and well.

We will have no future on the frontiers of science

---

4. For more on Operation Lightning Strike, see Marsha Freeman and Jeffrey Steinberg, "FBI Dirty Tricks Target NASA with Phony Scandals," *EIR*, Feb. 24, 1995, pp. 42-25. See also Gary Cartwright, "The Sting," *Texas Monthly*, August 1996.

5. See, for example, these contributions to the Sept. 16, 2016 issue of *EIR*: Helga Zepp-LaRouche, "The G-20 Summit: 'A Change of World-Historic Dimensions,' " pp. 5-11, and William Jones, "China Changes the Course of World History," pp. 12-18.

6. Lee eventually received $1.6 million from the federal government and media organizations in a civil suit for the leaking of his name to the press before any formal charges had been filed against him. Federal Judge James A. Parker blasted the Justice Department for misconduct and misrepresentations to the court.

unless we get rid of this noxious influence in our national life.

The American Spirit, from China and Russia

New international leadership is coming into being, making bold decisions to act for the future of mankind. As a feature of this process, a new era of space exploration is opening, prompted by the initiatives of China, Russia, and India, in cooperation with developing nations and their scientists and engineers. It is infectious! Yet here in the United States, we are still operating under the bankrupt Bush-Obama policies, bipartisan Congressional budget-cutting against NASA, and the FBI's continued intimidation of our nation's best potential leaders and scientists.

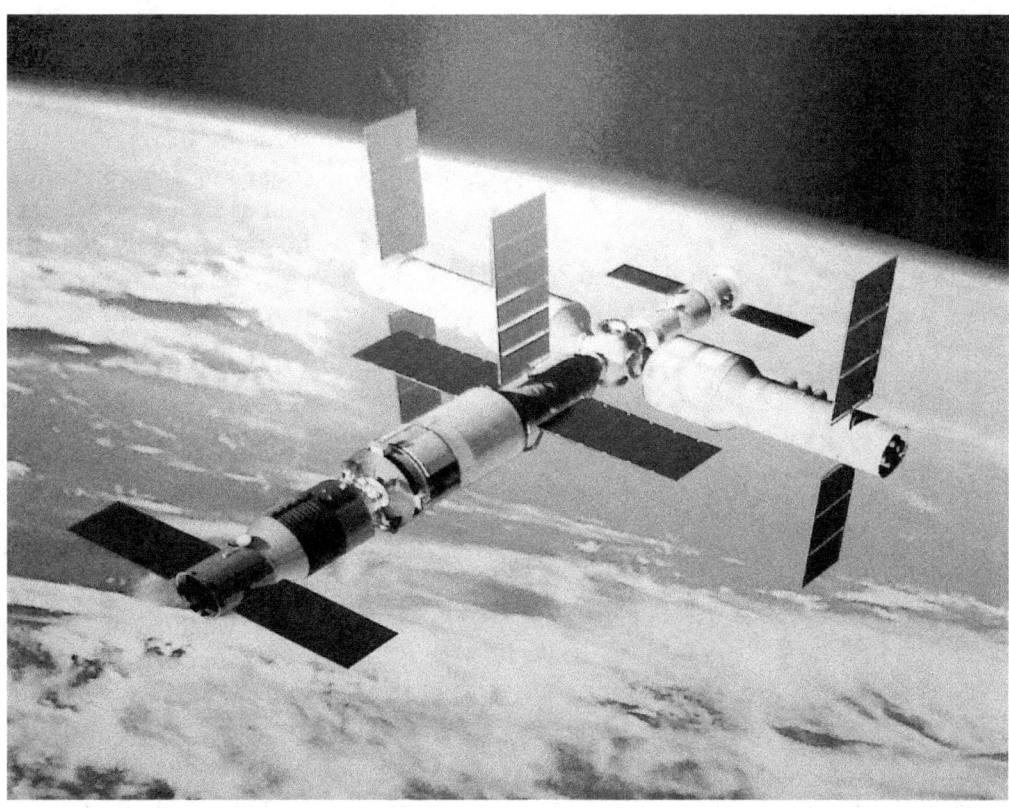

China.org

An artist's rendition of China's planned 60-ton, multi-module space station, set to be established in orbit by 2022.

Let us refresh ourselves and begin to recover some of the profound intention that lay behind the U.S. space program. Consider what President John F. Kennedy said, shortly before his assassination, in his singular address to the United Nations General Assembly in September 1963:

> Finally, in a field where the United States and the Soviet Union have a special capacity—in the field of space—there is room for new cooperation, for further joint efforts in the regulation and exploration of space. I include among these possibilities a joint expedition to the Moon. Space offers no problems of sovereignty; by resolution of this Assembly, the members of the United Nations have foresworn any claim to territorial rights in outer space or on celestial bodies, and declared that international law and the United Nations Charter will apply.
>
> Why, therefore, should man's first flight to the Moon be a matter of national competition?

Why should the United States and the Soviet Union, in preparation for such expeditions, become involved in immense duplications of research, construction, and expenditure? Surely we should explore whether the scientist and astronauts of our two countries—indeed of all the world—cannot work together in the conquest of space, sending someday in this decade to the Moon not the representatives of a single nation, but the representatives of all of our countries.[7]

There is still that spirit today, and it is coming most profoundly from China. It was just announced in June that China and the UN Office for Outer Space Affairs have agreed to collaborate in involving other, especially developing nations, in China's upcoming space station, of which the core module is to be launched in 2018. The European Space Agency and Russia's Roscosmos are already involved in talks with their Chinese counterparts. The agreement was presented by Ms. Wu

7. The text and audio recording of the speech are available, here. as is a video excerpt here.

Ping, Deputy of China's Manned Space Agency. Russia's Deputy Prime Minister Dmitry Rogozin, also speaking to reporters in June, stated, "This is a very promising sphere in whose development both the Russian and Chinese sides are interested.... This cooperation is of purely peaceful, civilian nature and will finally benefit the entire humankind rather than only the participating states."

Within the American scientific community itself, there is still the natural, human passion for scientific collaboration. Science is, after all, a dialogue across generations—across both time and space. Speaking at the International Astronautical Congress in August 2015, NASA Administrator Charles Bolden said he believed the ban on collaboration between the United States and China in space, banned by Congress since 2011, is temporary. Bolden, a former astronaut, stated, "My successor will have a different policy." The policy will change, Bolden said, because if not, in the future, "we'll be on the outside looking in." Xu Dazhe, Administrator of the China National Space Administration, responded succinctly: "China has no difficulties in our cooperation policies with other agencies."

EIRNS

Helga Zepp-LaRouche in conversation with Xu Dazhe, the Head of the Chinese space agency CNSA, at the International Aerospace Forum in Washington, D.C. in January, 2013.

III. 'Living Memorial' for 9/11 Victims

A 'Living Memorial' for All the Victims of 9/11

by Dennis Speed

The whole objection, however, of the immorality of poetry rests upon a misconception of the manner in which poetry acts to produce the moral improvement of man. Ethical science arranges the elements which poetry has created, and propounds schemes and proposes examples of civil and domestic life: nor is it for want of admirable doctrines that men hate, and despise, and censure, and deceive, and subjugate one another. But poetry acts in another and diviner manner. It awakens and enlarges the mind itself by rendering it the receptacle of a thousand unapprehended combinations of thought.

—Percy Bysshe Shelley
"A Defence of Poetry"

EIRNS/Don Clark

The Schiller Institute Chorus performed Mozart's Requiem, *and sang Spirituals* a capella *in Manhattan, New York, Sept. 10, 2016 in a living memorial for victims of the 9/11 attacks.*

The Schiller Institute Chorus performing Mozart's Requiem *in the Mass at St.Joseph's Co-Cathedral in Brooklyn, New York on Sept. 11, 2016. Soloists, left to right: Jay Baylon (bass-baritone), Everett Suttle (tenor), Mary Phillips (mezzo-soprano), and Indira Mahajan (soprano).*

Sept. 20—The 3,000 people that participated in one or more of the "Living Memorial" concerts held in New York City Sept. 9-12, experienced Percy Shelley's hypothesis first hand. The "awakening and enlarging of the mind itself," in confronting the crime of Sept. 11, 2001 through the mind of Wolfgang Amadeus Mozart's *Requiem,* was a successful thought-experiment that demonstrated the existence in the human soul of what the poet Friedrich Schiller has referred to as the quality of the Sublime.

This is not merely to babble, using what brainwasher T.W. Adorno, the inventor of "top 40" radio, would have called "the jargon of authenticity," to say that "the concerts were sublime." Contrary to the Congress for Cultural Freedom, the human response to true art and its power, is not based on taste or opinion.

Rather, in certain circumstances, an audience can be gripped, even apparently against its will, by a great composition, and its members thrust above themselves

to recognize the greatness that secretly inhabits their own souls. From the Bronx, to Manhattan, to Brooklyn, and finally in Morristown, New Jersey, a town that lost many of its citizens on 9/11, that elevation of the audience occurred in those concerts, and as a result, people left better than when they had entered.

The Schiller Institute's New York City Community Chorus was the vocal core of the concerts, which also featured soloists Indira Mahajan (soprano), Mary Phillips (mezzo-soprano), Everett Suttle (tenor) and Phillip Cutlip (bass-baritone). Soloist Jay Baylon replaced Cutlip in the Sunday Mass at St. Joseph's Co-Cathedral. The Foundation for the Revival of Classical Culture, which sponsored the performances, has since 2012 correctly insisted that performances of the Classical repertoire should occur at the "Verdi Pitch," or what the Foundation's originator and head, Lynn J. Yen, calls "the proper tuning"—a Middle C equal to 256 cycles per second (C-256).

About this matter, the *Brooklyn Reporter* online newspaper said: "The Foundation for the Revival of Classical Culture presented a special performance of Mozart's *Requiem*, a piece rarely performed during a Mass, according to the Diocese." It continued,

The Schiller Institute NYC Community Chorus, accompanied by a 42-piece orchestra and guest soloists, performed the *Requiem* at the 'Verdi tuning....'

'Proper Verdi tuning allows for the most transparent blend of the human voice with the instruments, and thus, maximum sonority,' said Lynn Yen, the executive director of the Foundation for the Revival of Classical Culture. 'To hear the Mozart *Requiem* at this pitch is to experience the transcendent power of sacred music—to experience the true glory of God and music.'

Diane Sare, co-founder of the chorus with John Sigerson, who conducted the four *Requiem* performances, had created the New York Community Chorus—originally a group that was to be based in New Jersey—as a "first response" to the "choke-hold" killing of Eric Garner in Staten Island in the Summer of 2014, and the killing of two policemen in Brooklyn in December of that same year. (The policemen were in fact killed during the chorus' first "maiden voyage" concert, performing selections from Handel's *Messiah* with instrumental accompaniment. When the singers finished, they were told what had happened while

EIRNS/Pavel Penov

Lynn Yen, founder and head of the Foundation for the Revival of Classical Culture speaks at the Sept. 10, 2016 performance in Manhattan, New York. The Foundation sponsored the four performances.

EIRNS/Karen Nafziger

The "Teardrop Memorial" presented to the United States by Russia and President Putin, as a memorial to the victims of the Sept. 11, 2001 attacks.

they were singing, and, shocked, fully committed themselves to the project.)

The problem Sare recognized, as a former Congressional candidate and longtime associate of *EIR* founder Lyndon LaRouche as well as a musician, was that political protest, or backlash against political protest, was worse than useless in the aftermath of the cultural despair that has descended upon the United States over the past fifteen years of Bush and Obama presidencies.

It was LaRouche who had raised the idea of a "Living Memorial" in the course of one of his weekly Manhattan dialogues, in responding to a veteran's question concerning how such commemorations might occur. Months prior, Sigerson had proposed, "if it were possible," that a Mozart *Requiem* performance might be done somewhere in the City. The "Living Memorial" idea was further concretized by the "discovery" by an individual visiting New York City, of a 100-foot-tall monument, called the "Tear Drop Memorial," dedicated by the people of Russia, and personally by Vladimir Putin in 2005, to the United States, its people, and the struggle against world terrorism.

The monument was "hiding in plain sight," directly across from the site of the World Trade Center's destruction, in Bayonne, New Jersey, and virtually never acknowledged. Former Speaker of the New Jersey Assembly Joseph Doria, the mayor of Bayonne at the time that the monument was first dedicated, said, "People have asked me why it was built by the Russians. And I explain: The Russians wanted the United States citizens to know that the entire world cried after 9/11 to see the desecration, and this slaughter of innocents for no purpose at all."

It was determined by the Foundation for the Revival of Classical Culture, including students that had just participated in a five-week long Summer-school, as well as parents, teachers, and members of service organizations, that everything would be done to allow everyone that wished to attend these concerts in New York City to do so, to be given that opportunity. The disquisition on the subject of immortality that is the dying Mozart's *Requiem,* would be presented in not one, but four performances, complete with a 42-piece orchestra and a chorus which at its smallest was 80 persons, and at its largest was 170.

The daunting Responsibility that would confront the ensemble in these four days, was that the performances would require the quality of the Sub-

EIRNS/Stuart Lewis

Firefighters of Battalion 57 of the New York Fire Department carried 23 flags to the mass at St. Joseph's Co-Cathedral on Sept. 11, 2016, in commemoration of the 23 firefighters from the Battalion who died on Sept. 11, 2001.

lime. An amateur chorus, coupled with a professional orchestra, soloists, and conductor, would have to deliver an effect not merely "credible" to the hearers, but one that would be life-changing. Life had, after all, on Sept. 11, 2001, been changed for millions forever that day, murderously. Was there a way to use music, for those that participated, either by listening, or performing, to defy "the triumph of the grave"?

Friedrich Schiller and 9/11

Friedrich Schiller's essay, "On The Sublime," contains this passage:

All nature acts according to reason; (man's) prerogative is merely, that he act according to reason with consciousness and will. All other things must; man is the being, who wills.

Precisely for this reason is (there) nothing so unworthy of man as to suffer violence, for vio-

lence annuls him. Who does it to us, disputes nothing less than our humanity; who suffers it in a cowardly manner, throws away his humanity.

Schiller goes on to say that the highest expression of the human will, is that case in which a man or woman willfully suffers violence in favor of preserving and advancing the idea of humanity as a whole. "To annihilate violence as a concept, however, is called nothing other than to voluntarily subject oneself to the same." In fact, that higher ideal of humanity was exactly what was upheld by many of the first responders—firemen, policemen, medical personnel, and volunteers—on that horrific day of 9/11.

For several reasons, the Mozart *Requiem* presented at St. Joseph's Co-Cathedral in Brooklyn was a particularly unique moment in American history, and not merely in music. The *Requiem* was performed as part of a full Catholic Mass, probably the first of its kind in the United States since January 1964, when a similar ceremony was conducted in honor of the slain John F. Kennedy at the request of his wife, Jacqueline, at Boston's Cathedral of the Holy Cross. The difference from even that occasion, though, was that this Sept. 11, though the *Requiem* was to be performed, the Mass was not itself a "requiem Mass ," because such a Mass cannot be performed on a Sunday, the day of Christ's resurrection in the Christian faith. Sunday cannot be a liturgical "day of death," but must needs be a day of affirmation of life. The "Gloria" from the Mozart Mass in D Minor, K. 65, was therefore added. That Mass also concluded with "Worthy Is The Lamb That Was Slain/ Amen," the end of Handel's Messiah, employed as the dismissal hymn.

This annual Brooklyn ceremony is dedicated to and attended by the firefighters of Battalion 57 of the Fire

EIRNS/Stuart Lewis

Bishop Nicholas DiMarzio (left) and Msgr. Kieran Harrington celebrated the Sept. 11, 2016 mass at St. Joseph's Co-Cathedral.

Department of New York, 23 of whose members had given their lives for their country on Sept. 11, 2001. Hundreds of firefighters attended. *The Tablet,* the diocesan newspaper, reported:

> Prior to the Mass, members of the Battalion, which includes five engine companies and one ladder company in Brooklyn, marched from Ground Zero in Manhattan, over the Brooklyn Bridge, to St. Joseph's Co-Cathedral, making stops at several firehouses along the way. They carried FDNY [New York Fire Department] flags, one for each of their fallen members. For the firefighters, the journey to Brooklyn served to symbolize the return home of their fallen comrades, said Firefighter Thomas Callahan, who delivered opening remarks at the church.

Bishop Nicholas DiMarzio and Msgr. Kieran Harrington concelebrated the Mass, attended by 1100-1200 people. Bishop DiMarzio's homily was remarkable for its direct emphasis on the idea of forgiveness. He pointed out that the firefighter fulfills not only the New Testament admonition, "Greater love than this, no man hath, that a man lay down his life for his friends." The firefighter does this for strangers, and even, sometimes, his enemies, and he does that every day, as a vocation. The inclusion of the *Requiem* as

part of the celebration of the Sunday Mass for Sept. 11 was suggested by Msgr. Harrington.

African-American Spirituals and 9/11

Diane Sare and her chorus are becoming leading defenders of the African-American Spiritual in the United States. Sare is privileged to have known and worked with the great Sylvia Olden Lee for about a decade. She also knows several of the late Ms. Lee's collaborators, such as mezzo-soprano Elvira Green, tenor and choral master Gregory Hopkins, the late William Warfield, and several others.

Increasingly, in many performances of Classical music in today's United States, the Spiritual should be performed, but only by competent choirs. The reason is that Americans can no longer hear, and usually confuse music with noise, electronic and non-electronic. The African-American Spiritual can provide a welcome antidote to that problem.

The words of the Spirituals are simple, but their meaning is not. The audience, hearing the least words possible, but with the historical drama of the triumph over slavery in America's 1861-65 conflict as an implicit backdrop, is taken beyond its "entertainment zone," its "comfort zone," and placed on the stage of the tragedy. It is the hard fought-for humanity present in that tragedy that is the province of those songs—not the songs of slaves, but of those that would be free even at the price of death. In this way, Americans are also given a gateway to what the intent was, for example, behind the operas of Giuseppe Verdi, or in this instance, the Mozart *Requiem.* Sare's chorus performed "Deep River," " When I was Sinkin' Down," "My Lord, What A Morning," and "Soon Ah Will Be Done," without accompaniment. The significance of the C=256 tuning was heard in the transparency of the voices relative to that of other choruses, which allows for the "inner voices" to be clearly heard without distortion.

The choral prelude was prerequisite to establishing an audience concentration-span, and audience "listening standard," before a note of Mozart were sung. This was particularly noticeable in the Saturday, Sept. 10 performance at St. Bartholomew's Church on Park

Avenue (Spirituals were not performed as part of the Sunday ceremony).

Soprano and vocal coach Carmela Altamura, who was unable to attend the concerts, made the following comment about about the "Living Memorial idea":

> Through music, and through the arts, and through the beauty and the harmony of the arts, man can easily reveal himself to his true Self. Man can find this through the arts, which are not always beautiful. This is also a part of man. Music has cacophony, it can have dissonance; that, too, is a revelation of the Self. In order to have harmony, you must recognize the difference between harmony and dissonance—the two go together, so man can choose.
>
> The horror of 9/11 is part of the dissonance, part of the darkness of man. We can also get to understand our darkness. It can reveal itself to us. There are some thoughts and emotions that man will not even want to reveal. Better to confront them and not push them aside, because only by recognizing them can we choose—do we have the freedom of choosing.
>
> The arts also bring us to this realization. So man, through the arts, can turn towards freedom, can turn towards the light, which elevates his soul to the highest achievement of a destiny of development—the highest level of expression.

Terry Strada, the head of "9/11 Families and Survivors United for Justice Against Terrorism," welcomed the ensemble and audience to the Morristown concert. Strada, who played the role of "unofficial Congressman" in the unanimous passage of the Justice Against the Sponsors of Terrorism Act (JASTA) by the House of Representatives and the Senate, wanted it to be known that it was possible to fight and win justice. She also

EIRNS/Torrie Hall

Terry Strada, the head of "9/11 Families and Survivors United for Justice Against Terrorism," spoke at the Schiller Institute performance at the Presbyterian Church in Morristown, N.J., Sept. 12, 2016.

said, "I thank you very much for taking the time to listen to me, and now I'm so honored to have these wonderful musicians. I have heard them practice. You are in for a treat. This is going to be a very wonderful time now for us to just transcend ourselves from the evil, to a higher place—to a place where Good is. I believe Good will win, and I thank you for coming." [applause]

'The Power of the Beautiful'

More than 100 people indicated their willingness to become members of the Schiller Institute Chorus, by the end of the four-day period. The Foundation for the Revival of Classical Culture received many favorable comments transmitted to their website. Student volunteers of the Foundation, who had distributed leaflets and concert announcements every day for a ten-day period at Lincoln Center, also reported that many youth, as young as twelve and thirteen, were actively discussing how to form a youth chorus in the Bronx. There, state legislator José Rivera, who had been, together with several other prominent figures in the Bronx, involved on the ground floor in encouraging the inclusion of the Bronx in this work, was in attendance. He remarked that, although people might think that he "was only listening to Salsa," things are a lot different than

The Schiller Institute Chorus performance of Mozart's Requiem *at the Presbyterian Church in Morristown, N.J.*

they might seem.

People, as poet Friedrich Schiller once wrote, "are born for that which is better." The concert program essay, "The Power of the Beautiful," concluded:

The struggle of the human being to become better, to discover his/her purpose in the universe, the struggle to make life matter, does not require violence; it requires the abolition of violence. It requires the willful and deliberate rejection of beast-like reactive emotions largely based in fear and rage, and the conscious acceptance of the responsibility to 'institute government among men,' established to nurture that creative human identity that is the birthright of all people, for all time. Classical music's greatest composers create, utilizing various forms— string quartets, symphonies, and solo works— new discoveries in time, new human forms of nature, new realizations whose physical power to change the world by provoking the human mind to lift itself 'above the heavens,' can change the very destiny of the universe itself. In the works of the greatest composers, we can hear, experience and partake in that inner self-advancement, to express and communicate more and more perfectly the truth of that which is all around us: Life is simultaneously a gift, and the very force of the universe itself. It is free, but necessary; it is unique, but infinitely reproducible; it is limited in the individual, but limitless in the species. Life is beautiful, and bountiful.

That is the song of the future that we hear in the *Requiem* of Wolfgang Amadeus Mozart. That is the means whereby the crime of September 11, 2001, and its even more horrific ongoing consequences can be expiated from the world. There was a reason that the walls of Jericho 'came a tumblin' down,' and it was not the superior force of arms, but of voices—the voices of those who, through Beauty, had proceeded to free their souls, and therefore their nation. So shall it be with us.

Performing Mozart's *Requiem*

EIR interviewed Schiller Institute Director John Sigerson on Sept. 20, 2016.

EIR: How did your approach to directing and balancing the orchestra and chorus in the *Requiem* differ from that which we often hear as the approach to Mozart's work in locations such as the "Mostly Mozart" performed at Lincoln Center?

John Sigerson: It's been many years since I've listened to Mostly Mozart at Lincoln Center, so I don't wish to say anything about that particular ensemble today. But I will say that ever since the 1980s, I've noticed a marked shift in the attitude of many professional string players in how they believe they are expected to play works of Mozart and other composers of his era. Instead of the rich, passionate bowstrokes typified by Lyndon LaRouche's friend Norbert Brainin, who led the Amadeus Quartet for so many years, string players began to believe what was required of them for Mozart, was shorter bowstrokes and very little vibrato, a practice which tends to destroy the beautiful legato line which is the hallmark of great *bel canto* singing.

At the same time, what I can fairly describe as a false dichotomy developed between "instrumental" and "vocal" performance. In his written works, LaRouche has often inveighed against the absurdity of this dichotomy, and has rightly insisted that the fount of all Classical performance is the well-trained *bel canto* singing voice. What he said resonated with me personally, too, because in my student time at Juilliard, I was fortunate enough to study with the great contrabass soloist Gary Karr, who insisted that even on that seemingly grumbly instrument, one must sing passionately and expressively, and not just saw away at the notes.

This kind of dichotomy goes even further back to the conflict between Wilhelm Furtwängler and Arturo Toscanini regarding the relationship of the musician to

EIRNS/Stuart Lewis

John Sigerson conducting the Schiller Institute Chorus performance of Mozart's Requiem *at the St. Joseph Co-Cathedral in Brooklyn, N.Y. on Sept. 11, 2016.*

the musical score. Whereas Toscanini insisted that his purpose was to interpret as exactly as possible what is in the written score, Furtwängler countered that the performer must always strive to re-create the work in such a way that listeners are drawn into the mind of its creator, and that therefore the performance must focus not so much on the notes themselves, as what is "behind the notes." And of course, I am on Furtwängler's side on that.

EIR: How did the Sunday performance, embedded in the Catholic liturgy, differ from the others?

Sigerson: What we planned jointly with the Co-Cathedral of St. Joseph in Brooklyn on Sunday, September 11 was in fact a unique experiment, integrating the Mozart *Requiem* with a Sunday Catholic Mass. The Requiem Mass service is generally never performed on Sunday, and so in the course of a number of meetings with Msgr. Kieran Harrington, the Parish Rector of the Cathedral, we fashioned a sequence which was congenial to the performance requirements of our chorus and orchestra, while it adhered to the liturgical requirements at the same time.

EIRNS/Stuart Lewis

The Schiller Institute Chorus, accompanying orchestra, and Conductor John Sigerson at the St. Joseph Co-Cathedral in Brooklyn.

One question that immediately came up in those discussions, was the *Requiem*'s lack of a "Gloria" section as required by the liturgy. This I solved by inserting a "Gloria" from one of Mozart's earlier masses, namely his *Missa Brevis in D minor*, which is in the same key and mode as the *Requiem*. And it came as a nice, not so surprising surprise, that at the very end of this little "Gloria," Mozart inserts a little proto-fugal theme which foreshadows the *Requiem*'s main "Kyrie eleison" fugal subject—which, in turn, harks back to J.S. Bach's and Handel's magnificent work with this same theme.

Transparency and Tuning

EIR: How did the C=256 tuning change the transparency exhibited in the performances?

Sigerson: Just to be clear: We performed at the "Verdi tuning" of A=432 Hz, which is slightly higher than the A=430.5 Hz required for setting Middle C at exactly 256 Hz. Both of these slightly different tunings work fine with the vocal registration that Verdi was concerned about, however I have tended to stick with A=432 Hz because it's marginally easier to get an orchestra with modern instruments to play at that pitch. For example, in our performance the clarinets were right at their limit, and I doubt they could have played in tune even one cycle lower. As far as transparency is concerned, we are still at the very start of being able to construct an orchestra that can play really well and easily on modern instruments (that is, not "period" instruments) at the Verdi tuning. We still have a great number of technological problems to solve in this regard, and until they are solved, everything is quite experimental.

But as for the chorus, there is definitely greater transparency, not only because the vocal registration "works" (even though many singers in the chorus are only half aware of where their registers sit), but because there is a certain "ease" or "rightness" which sets in once singers become accustomed to singing at this tuning. And this ease of delivery results in greater transparency—and a lot more fun!

EIR: Is there in fact any appreciable difference, any difference which is important, between the first sections of the *Requiem*, and those composed by Franz Süssmayr after Mozart's death?

Sigerson: For anyone who has seriously studied this work, there is a definite difference between the genius shown in the sections by Mozart, and the respectfully workmanlike completions by Süssmayr. For me personally, the difference becomes most palpable in that indescribable moment where Mozart, near death, breaks off after the first bars of the "Lacrymosa," which had to be completed by Süssmayr only based on Mozart's verbal indications.

Another example is the "Benedictus." As beautiful as Süssmayr's composition of this section is, I can't help thinking that had Mozart been able to compose it, it would have had something much more profound, perhaps foreshadowing the incredible "Benedictus" of Beethoven's *Missa Solemnis*.

EIR: There was a notable difference in the attack delivered at the very beginning of the *Requiem* performances, and there was also a significant difference in how you conducted and how the chorus sang sections such as the "Lacrymosa." Why was that?

Sigerson: The opening back-and-forth in the strings has to evoke the deliberately slow, solemn, somewhat hesitant steps as one enters the cathedral to participate in the *Requiem*. Both the tempo and the slightly lengthened bowstrokes must reflect that. I almost succeeded in getting this, but lack of rehearsal time prevented me from getting exactly what I wanted. The "Lacrymosa" is so emotionally compelling, that I concluded that a thunderous "Amen" at the end—which is the way it is commonly done—tends to undermine the total effect. "Calming down" the ending "Amen" has the effect of allowing us to wipe away the tears that inevitably flow if we allow ourselves to be moved.

The *Requiem,* the Spirituals, and *Messiah*

EIR: How did you think the combination of African-American spirituals, Mozart's *Requiem*, and selections from Handel's *Messiah* worked?

Sigerson: Diane Sare, who conducted those pieces, is committed to reviving the *correct* performance of these spirituals, many of which were arranged by collaborators of Antonin Dvorak during his extended stay in the United States. They are a crucial, Classical antidote to "gospel" singing's tendency to drift into banality and plain bad singing. Similar to the German *Lied* for German-speakers, these spirituals strike a deep chord in the soul, with their assertion of the fundamental distinction between man and beast. And for these reasons, they fit perfectly with our intention with the Mozart *Requiem*.

As for Handel, Mozart venerated the man, as did Beethoven, and even made an arrangement of *Messiah* to suit Viennese tastes. I don't think he would have any problem adding Handel's great D major "Amen" chorus at the end of Mozart's own unfinished work in D minor. After all, Beethoven's Ninth Symphony works the same way, beginning in D minor and ending the final "Ode to Joy" movement with a tumultuous D major.

Will the Next Beethoven Be an American?

José Vega interviewed Diane Sare on Sept. 18. José Vega has just graduated from high school, and is a youth activist for the Foundation for the Revival of Classical Culture. Diane Sare is a member of the LaRouche PAC Policy Committee, and the choral director of the Schiller Institute's New York City Community Chorus.

José Vega: First things first. Where did the chorus come from? The idea of it,— why start a chorus in New York City?

Diane Sare: Well, we have a chorus,— the Schiller Institute has had choruses for a long time, and we have had a small chorus in New Jersey for a number of years. What

EIRNS/Stuart Lewis
Diane Sare conducting members of the Schiller Institute Chorus in Manhattan in January 2015, shortly after the chorus-building process began.

happened was that in the Winter of 2014 you had the situation in St. Louis with the police shooting of a young, unarmed African-American, and the riots that followed, and then the case here in Staten Island with the strangling of Eric Garner. After the grand jury came back and said that there was nothing indictable [in the Garner case], there was a great deal of anger, justified anger, but not yet to the point to which various elements wanted to fan it. That is, we thought there was a danger that New York would be divided against police, against the African-American population,— the typical divisions that are played, frankly, when you have an economic collapse.

We decided to do a sing-along of Handel's *Messiah* at that time, which we pulled together in six days, and to my surprise, about one hundred people showed up to sing. In the course of organizing it, I found some old friends of ours, particularly people like the accompanist Robert Wilson. It turns out that he had been the accompanist to Carlo Bergonzi, and knew about the Schiller Institute since 1988 in Milan,— our campaign for the lower tuning. It was clear there was really a great poten-

tial to pull something together. After that sing-along, someone who attended said, "I would like to sing in your chorus, but I don't want to go to New Jersey. Why don't you organize a community chorus in Manhattan?" Given that Lyndon LaRouche had just launched the Manhattan Project, it seemed like the natural thing to do. So I decided to create a community chorus in New York City, and that was the origin of it.

Ending Violence through Music

Vega: So, basically it's about bringing people together, ending violence through music. Is that where the concert came from, also,— the one we recently held at four different churches, the Mozart *Requiem*?

Sare: Yes, and I would say, in a sense, our chorus was lucky to participate in this event sponsored by the Foundation for the Revival of Classical Culture,— and I would say the question of ending violence is not simply the idea of "let's not be violent." The question of ending violence, of why shouldn't human beings be violent, is polemical; a lot of animals are quite violent. The point is that human beings are not animals. What you see in the music of the great classical composers, and particularly for the United States, the traditional African-American spiritual, is a demonstration that human beings are not animals, and are, as Schiller said, "born for something better."

The African-American Spiritual

Vega: That leads me to my next question. Why use the spirituals before the *Requiem*?

Sare: Well, of course one could say that the *Requiem* stands alone. It is an extraordinary, beautiful piece,— but what many people said to me afterwards is that the spirituals prepared them to actually hear the *Requiem* in its intent. I think, especially in a moment like this, when you have a President of the United States who is committed to every act of violence and a complete disregard for human life, and a country therefore which is reflecting that with more and more killings, more and more crimes of human beings against each other, and a culture of despair generally, the thing about the spirituals is that,— because they are really American, they are in English, they come from the United States. They come from this nation, and they express something very powerful. That is, they were sung by people who were under absolutely hideous conditions of brutality, yet there is not a shred of brutality that is reflected in this music. The spirituals are, in that respect, sublime, because they express a quality of humanity which overcomes the brutality and degradation that people were forced to suffer.

So in a sense, I think there is a great potential, and you really saw it at these events, that the population can really resonate with this music. It is very moving, and while on the one hand it seems very simple,— the words are simple, there is not counterpoint in the sense you would see it in a Bach fugue or the Mozart *Requiem*,— yet there is a certain richness to the voices and the interaction of them, or the harmony, I guess you could say,— but it's a way to really reach the American people at this time. I think that's extremely

Antonin Dvorak in New York City in 1904.

significant, and you could see that in the response of many people in the audience to the spirituals.

The Next Beethoven

Vega: Okay, well, I think you did succeed in that. Is there anything else you would like to say?

Sare: I would like to say that when Dvorak came to the United States, he recognized in the melodies of these songs, the spirituals,— and also, he said, in the native American music,— that they contain everything that is necessary for, I think the words were, "a great and noble school of American classical music,"—very much in the way Brahms had found it in the folk music of Europe. Dvorak, who was a collaborator of Brahms, attempted to establish an American Conservatory of Music with largely African-American musicians. Because of the setback during Reconstruction, the backlash to that, the British imperial racists, Jim Crow, etc., and then later, in 1913, the revival of the Ku Klux Klan,— what happened is this National Conservatory process was crushed.

But you had a handful of people,— and ironically, many of them worked out of Manhattan. That is where Dvorak was. People like our accompanist, Robert Wilson, worked with some of the people who were students of this process directly, as did some of the people I have recently come into contact with as a result of this work, like the choral conductor, singer and music professor, Dr. Eugene Simpson, who worked as accompanist and as a singer with Hall Johnson for the last eleven years of Hall Johnson's life. Johnson was one of the arrangers of the spirituals that we did. William Dawson was another one. What we are tapping into, in a sense, is a legacy which was to have become an American Conservatory of Music, a national movement in the United States for classical music. I think that may be the most important aspect of this. It is just the beginning of something which potentially will grow to be much greater after we have had a generation or two of excellent musicians. Maybe the next Beethoven will be in the United States.